Leisure Arts 27

Painting
Dogs in
Watercolour
Sally Michel

SEARCH PRESS

Wellwood North Farm Road Tunbridge Wells

Introduction

There can be no other group of animals which shares so close a relationship, and displays such disparity of size and shape, as the domestic dog. For example St Bernards and chihuahuas, deerhounds and Pekingese, all are members of a single species, and the differences between them are all the result of human interference in their affairs. How lucky we are that they are almost without exception friendly, loyal, cheerful and companionable, make few demands on their owners, and are quite happy to let us draw and paint them. This activity demands from the artist a wide range of subject and technique — every colour from black to white, pale yellow to red, every possible shade of brown; every kind of coat from satin to thick wool, glossy waves and tight curls, physiques ranging from one more slender than cats to one nearly the size of a Shetland pony. Clearly one needs to master a variety of styles, to use colour and brushes to convey many different characteristics; confining one's artistic activity to this one subject by no means indicates monotony of effect.

The materials needed are much the same as for any other subject, though of course some colours are used in large quantities; others while absolutely necessary, will be used only a little at a time. Lamp black, burnt sienna, and yellow ochre are again and again used in varying mixtures, but blues, violets and reds are needed to mix the subtly varied tones of the coats of different breeds — and of course backgrounds are in effect landscapes or interiors, and require a less restricted palette. In addition to the first three pigments mentioned, I use pthalocyanine blue, winsor yellow, winsor violet, quinacridone pink (permanent rose). These will supply most of the colours needed, though a deeper yellow such as cadmium, and a bright red (cadmium light) can be very useful.

To start with, it is not necessary to buy a large number of brushes, but it is desirable to have at least one fairly large one for background washes, two or three of medium sizes, and one or two really small sizes, 0 or 1, for fine details such as whiskers, which need to be of good quality.

A small light drawing-board — simply a piece of 3-ply about 12in. by 16in. (30cm by 40cm), with the corners rounded — is easier to work on than the usual heavier ½ inch board. Plenty of inexpensive paper for the numerous sketches and studies essential for animal work, and a variety of rag papers, hand-made or mould-made, for finished paintings, pencils and a soft rubber, complete one's requirements.

Anatomy and physique

Portraying any animal is, obviously, a matter of studying its appearance, deciding what are its essential characteristics, and setting them down in concrete form with accuracy and understanding. Some study of the anatomy can be particularly helpful in showing the differences and the similarities of very dissimilar dogs. The drawings on page 3 show some of what underlies the outward appearance, and demonstrate how the skeleton has had its proportions changed by selective breeding. The two breeds compared in each case started from the same point; the upper diagrams show a standard 'normal' shape, the lower ones, what modifications have been made by a long succession of carefully chosen matings. The shortening of the dachshund's legs is such that the long leg bones consist of little more than their two ends, the middle section having been reduced to almost nothing. Nevertheless, the relationship between the two is still very clear.

Alterations to the shape of dogs originated with the purpose of fitting them for particular uses, and most often

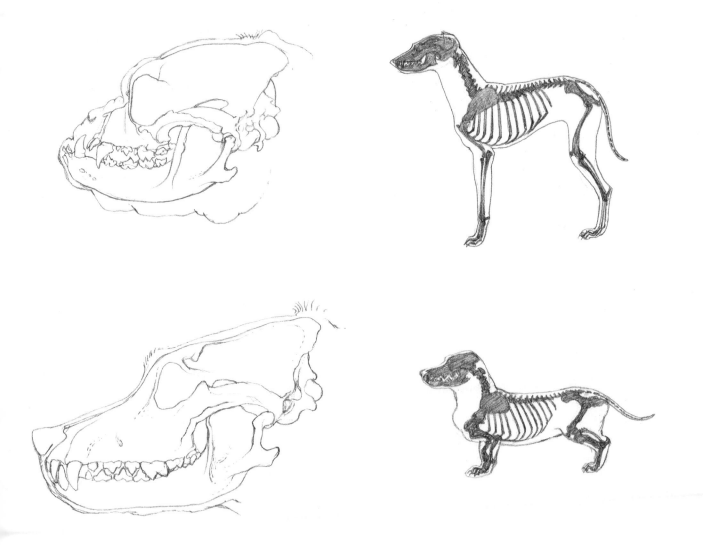

resulted in a sensible build and pleasing appearance. But when these uses are no longer relevant, and the standards are set mainly for competing in shows, appearance is valued above performance, and characteristics tend to become exaggerated, sometimes, unhappily, at the expense of health. Compare present-day champions with the forebears of a century ago (many photographs of these exist) and the process is clearly seen; short legs are shorter, pushed-back noses are now nearly as far back as the eyes,

long coats now reach the floor. Look at the diagram of the bulldog's skull; originally the intention was to enable the dog to grip a lump of bull without stopping up its nostrils. Early in this century, the nostrils were roughly half-way between the front teeth and the eyes; now, when few bulldogs need to have their noses anywhere but at the front, they are as far back as they will go, and the dogs snuffle and grunt.

Fur

The hair of dogs can be soft and fluffy, smooth and hard, or long and silky, all needing different treatment in watercolour. A principle to follow is that a smooth surface reflects light variably, so is depicted with juxtapositions of deep and light areas of tone, which give an impression of shiny smoothness, as in the example; curved brush strokes are used to show wavy hair. Soft fluffy hair can be shown by putting a wash on to dampened paper, so that the changes of tone are gradual, and the edges of the form are softened. Separate brush strokes can depict both coarse hairs, or locks of hair.

Eyes, ears and noses

All these features have complex and interesting shapes, and careful examination and drawing of them is necessary. Remember that eyes are spherical, and although only part of the sphere shows between the eyelids, it continues under the skin; remember that the part of the eye which shows is curved — when you are aware of such facts it is easier to draw convincingly.

Feet

The general rule is that dogs have five toes on their front feet — one a dew claw, analogous to a thumb, on the inside of the paw, and further back — and four on the back feet. In fact, there are exceptions; some dogs have only the four front toes on the forefoot, and the "thumb" is degenerate, with the claw not firmly attached. These dew claws are often removed in puppyhood, as they will otherwise be very likely to catch in things, and can cause painful injury to the dog, sometimes even being pulled right off. It is useful to examine and handle the feet, to help one understand their structure and range of movement.

Mongrels

The origins of the dog on this page are a mystery, but he is as cheerful, faithful and affectionate as any other dog.

The posture in this drawing was chosen from a number of sketches made from life; a basic wash of mixed burnt sienna and yellow ochre was worked into it before drying with a deeper colour to represent its rough coat and structure on the head and legs. Once this was dry the nose, eyes, collar and address tag were added.

The white dog is a pen drawing with a small amount of watercolour — the pen line suits the subject, whose outstanding characteristic is the coat of longish disordered curls: the fine line indicates the shape of these without falsifying the light tone.

The importance of drawing your subject

Whatever medium is intended for carrying out a painting, it must start with drawing. After years of experience, an artist may base his picture on a sketch so apparently slight that it seems almost as if the drawing stage is being by-passed. For this to be done successfully, careful study and observation must have been carried out in the past, over many years, so that the artist's thorough stored knowledge of the subject enables him to sum up very quickly the essential facts of the model before him, and to add these to what is already in his memory, to produce a true and completely understood presentation of what is there. Until this study has been done, it is as well to spend as much time as you can on drawing, and on the careful exploratory looking which is its necessary preliminary and accompaniment. Even if you have no immediate intention of doing a painting, no time spent on drawing is wasted; carry a sketch book with you, and draw whenever possible. Practice in drawing, on any subject, increases your ability to draw any other subject, so that even if the result appears to be of little significance, it has a beneficial effect on your general ability. By filling sketch books with drawings of many different animals you are building up your knowledge of their structure and habits, and also a useful record to refer to for later work. Do not be disheartened at the apparent impossibility of completing any one drawing — even the smallest sketch can be useful. Start another drawing if your subject moves — you may well later have a chance to go back to the first one. Keep all your drawings, however incomplete; make written notes about colours, behaviour, the age and sex of the animal and anything else that contributes to your knowledge. Label and date all your drawings, not forgetting to include the year. Try to draw from different viewpoints, and pay attention to the structure of eyes, feet, and ears.

Alsatian puppy: demonstration (pages 8 & 9)

Original size: 225mm sq./9in. sq
Paper: Mould-made Whatman 180gsm/90lb.

The young Alsatian, past the stage of infancy but still a puppy in behaviour at about six months of age, does not stay still for long except when asleep. Many quick drawings were made, and several were combined to supply the basis of the chosen pose; one drawing showed the entire body and legs, so that nothing was invented. The position of the head was taken from another drawing in which the body was incomplete.

Stage 1

The final drawing is done from life, working over a basic re-drawing of the first sketches. It is not necessary to see the dog in an identical position — that was obtained at the first sitting, and now only needs to be developed into a firm pencil study by means of constant reference to the animal.

Stage 2

The eyes are given their base-colour of mixed burnt sienna and yellow; the background is wetted all over; a mixture of pthalocyanine blue, cadmium yellow light, and Payne's grey gives the desired greyish green, and is used to build up a preliminary tone around the form of the dog, although the final tone will be adjusted later.

Stage 3

When the background colour is absolutely dry, a ground-tone of mixed yellow ochre and burnt sienna is washed over the dog, varying from very pale to a warm brown on the head and other parts, where extra burnt sienna is added to the still damp wash. The background tone is built up with the grey-green, with extra Payne's grey added.

Stage 1

Stage 2

Stage 3

Stage 4 — the finished painting

A wash of lamp black, varying from thick to very thin, is put over all those parts of the dog where the coat is black or where black hairs overlie the brown; some ultra-marine on the flank gives the light reflected by the glossy black hair. A thin black wash is put on the pads, and used for details of dark hairs; light hairs are defined with opaque yellowish white. Details on eyes and muzzle are defined in black, and highlights touched with opaque white and grey. The final tone of the background can be built up a little more if wished.

Stage 4 — the finished painting

Capturing moving dogs

While one may think of a dog in motion as one which is walking, running or leaping, or otherwise proceeding from one place to another, there are other kinds of movement, which may provide interest in a picture; rolling, scratching, or standing up on hind legs, for instance: a few of these are shown on these pages. As these movements can change rapidly, it is helpful to watch and observe the dog, to sum up in one's mind the general character of the action, to decide what stage of a movement will convey it most tellingly, and then set it down quickly and without lingering over details. These can be added later by means of referring to the required parts of the dog at leisure and drawing these in greater detail over the foundation already established.

Old English sheepdog: demonstration <small>(pages 12 & 13)</small>

Original size: 290 x 222mm/11½ x 8¾in.
Paper: Saunders 300gsm/140lb.

The shaggy coat and general build of this dog seem to make it a suitable subject for a very free, quick treatment. Inside the long thick coat is a large normally shaped dog, but the waving locks of hair are what fill the view.

Stage 1

First draw the figure of the dog on an absorbent medium-rough paper. The grey parts of the dog — ear, back, and haunch — are then given a freely brushed wash of slightly bluish grey.

    The whole shape of the dog is then outlined with curly brush strokes of masking fluid; this process is continued over all those parts of the dog which I want to keep white or very pale.

Stage 2

A very pale, yellow-grey is used on the parts which, though in light, need a little tone to show the individual locks of white fur. So more masking fluid is added to protect this colour, and another medium-grey wash is then put on to the shadowed parts of the dog's face, head and body.

Stage 3

I make sure that the dog-shape is protected by masking fluid sufficiently far in from its edges to permit the background colour to be brushed on with considerable speed, and then prepare two mixtures of colour: one of manganese blue and a little Payne's grey, the other of Winsor violet, Payne's grey and a little ultramarine.

Stage 1

Stage 2

These are applied in bold free strokes, diagonally, in such a way as to let both colours be seen and to mix and, in places, to drag over the paper and let a little of it remain uncovered.

Stage 4 — the finished painting

It is essential that the work is allowed to dry thoroughly before the solidified masking fluid is rubbed off, otherwise it may damage the surface of the paper. When this was done, the dog was revealed, standing out cleanly against the background. A very dark bluish grey was used for some more shaggy locks on the grey parts of the body and ear, and the black end of the nose added.

This treatment has the quite pleasing effect of giving the picture the appearance of a print.

Stage 3

Stage 4 — the finished painting

Spaniels

The spaniels and their related breed have been bred mainly for retrieving, and are cabable of carrying things in their mouths without inflicting damage; they also tend to plunge into water whenever the opportunity arises. There are many breeds of spaniel — the cockers, British and American, springer, clumber and water-spaniels; King Charles spaniels and papillons, and many others; the setters are in effect tall spaniels; retrievers and labradors may be regarded as related breeds.

They have silky, often wavy or curly coats, long soft ears, rather domed heads and soft baggy mouths. The drawings are studies of various spaniels; the illustration is of an English cocker spaniel; here again, much of the work in the picture consists of putting in the hair, which is much softer and smoother than the samoyed's, and wavy.

Dog, walking: demonstration (pages 16 & 17)

Original size: 185 x 375mm/7¼ x 15in.
Paper: Saunders 180gsm/90lb.

The gait of a dog walking on its own is quite different from that of a dog on a lead. The golden labrador in this picture ambles along sampling the interesting scents left by previous travellers.

Stage 1

As always, the drawing is of prime importance; it is not essential to include a lot of detail as long as you have detailed studies to work from, or the living animal. It is vital that what you draw is in the right place.

Stage 2

The background is left vague, simple washes of colour to suggest a rough path and verdure. These are applied to previously wetted paper in bands of yellow-green, with darker bluer green above, and greyish brown below.

Stage 3

When this is thoroughly dry a light wash of yellow ochre is put all over the dog — much paler on the inside of the far hind leg, and on the lower parts of the face and neck; deepened and warmed up with added burnt sienna on the crown, ear, neck, shoulders, rump and tail.

Stage 4 — the finished painting

All the sharp detail is added now; a black wash, with some burnt sienna in it, is used to model the structure of the face, mouth, eye and nose, building up with a less watery mixture, finally at almost full strength to give the head considerable prominence. Further washes of warm brown are used on the ear, neck, shoulders and tail, where deeper coloured hair overlies the pale coat. Fine brush marks indicate the lie of the hair, and point up the details of ear, eye, and paws.

Stage 1

Stage 2

Stage 3

Stage 4 — the finished painting

Hounds

One tends to count as one group a number of dogs called hounds of various kinds, which are used in packs to hunt their quarry by scent: bloodhounds, foxhounds, harriers, beagles, basset and other hounds. Bloodhounds were originally used for hunting deer. They are used for finding people now, of course, and have the ability to follow a scent as much as four days old. This reveals how completely different from ours is a dog's sensitivity to smells.

The most complicated part of the drawing is the bloodhound's face with its swags and folds of skin. Apart from this it is a matter of an all-over wash of light yellowish brown, with a black washed over it after it is dry, and a stronger mixture of brown to define the modelling of legs, feet and body.

18

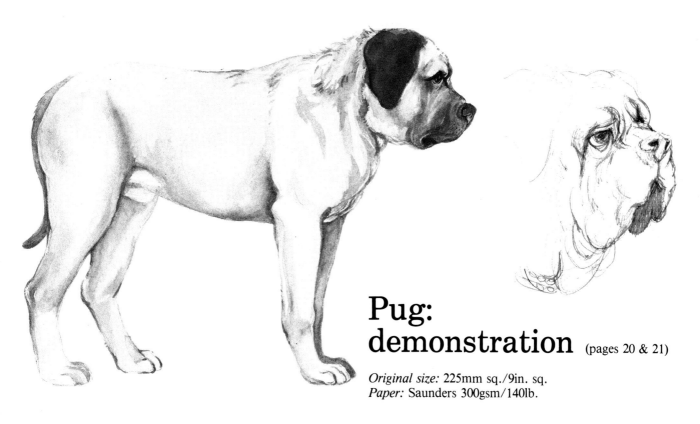

Pug: demonstration (pages 20 & 21)

Original size: 225mm sq./9in. sq.
Paper: Saunders 300gsm/140lb.

Stage 1

This painting has a simple wash background, as I do not want to distract attention from the complications of the folds of skin on the dog's head and shoulders. These must be carefully drawn before one starts to put on the colour.

Stage 2

The background is wetted with clean water, and the colour applied — a mixture of blues: manganese, cobalt and ultramarine — light around the head, darker where it adjoins the lighter-toned body.

Stage 3

A very pale wash of yellow ochre is put over the whole dog, some stronger yellow ochre is added along its back and on its tail.

Mastiffs

Mastiffs are one of the oldest breeds of dog — a dog very similar to our present-day mastiff is shown in Assyrian reliefs. Most large, heavily-built dogs can be classified as varieties of mastiff: St Bernards, Pyrenean and Bernese mountain dogs, Great Danes, and Newfoundlands; bull mastiffs, bulldogs and boxers might also be included in this group.

The mastiff in the picture is short-coated, so that its powerful heavy build is clearly seen; the skin on its head is looser and hangs heavily round its lower jaw, and above its eyes. The picture required careful drawing, but the watercolour treatment is straightforward and direct, with simple washes over the drawing, and a little reinforcement of details with a fine brush.

Stage 1

Stage 2

Stage 3

Stage 4 — the finished painting

A thin wash of black over the yellow ochre gives some modelling to the body and legs, and the rolls of loose skin around the shoulders and neck. This is built up in stages to a full-strength black, to define the folds on the face and the black mask and ears, and the eyes, in which a little burnt sienna and black has been used for the irises.

Opaque white mixed with a little yellow ochre and black is used to define the fur on face, chest and abdomen. A light opaque grey then defines the details of nose and mouth, and the folds around the eyes. A touch of almost pure white outside the irises helps to enhance the characteristically worried expression.

Stage 4 — the finished painting

Terriers

The terriers form a very large group, varied in build and ranging in size from Airedales (not often seen nowadays) as big as retrievers, down to Yorkshire terriers, minute but well able to speak up for themselves. By definition terriers were bred for digging out unfortunate animals which had taken refuge underground. They come in almost any variation of colour. Legs vary in length from long, as in Airedales, to almost none, as in Sealyhams.

The picture here is of a wire-haired fox terrier — much the same animal as a smooth terrier but with a wiry springy weather-proof coat. Comparison between the two pictures may illustrate that, when drawing a long-coated dog, one must remain aware that what lies under the hair is an animal with muscles, bones and tendons.

Although at a cursory glance such an animal may look shapeless, and the arrangement of hair disordered, the position of each lock of hair is determined by its place on the solid dog beneath. Thorough study of the animal reveals this, and careful drawing will show both the nature of the coat and the form of the dog inside it.

Dog, digging: demonstration (pages 24 & 25)

Original size: 180 x 220mm/7 x 8⅝in.
Paper: Saunders 180gsm/90lb.

This picture again uses masking solution but to a lesser extent than in the Old English sheepdog painting.

The way in which I use it is a little different; it again defines the edges of the animal, so that a wash can be put freely over the background, leaving a clean edge, and leaving the brown and white dog to stand out against the green and sandy-coloured setting, yet defining the character of the subject's coat. The short, rough coat seems best conveyed by the use of fine brush marks, in brown and grey on pale yellow-brown and white patches of hair, and also, by using opaque white, with a counter-change of tone, pale yellowish and white brush strokes on these dark and middle-toned areas.

Stage 1

The dog (that most dedicated digger, a Jack Russell terrier) is drawn carefully, and the features of the background only lightly indicated. With all these pictures, the animals have been very carefully drawn beforehand, often more than once, and the final result carefully traced so that the drawing can be reproduced without harming the delicate surface of the paper.

I then apply the masking fluid all round the edges of the animal, with indications of hairs where these interrupt the outline, as on the head, neck, tail and elbow.

Stage 2

The daisies in the grass are then stopped out, and all this work with masking fluid is then allowed to dry thoroughly before I embark on the painting of the background. The far background is painted into wet paper — a pale lemon wash with a hint of phthalocyanine blue, above it a dull green obtained by adding Payne's grey. While this dries, space can be left for the patch of grass behind the dog, and a ground of yellow ochre with burnt umber washed across at the level of the dog's feet.

Stage 3 & 4

A deeper yellow-green (cadmium lemon, phthalocyanine blue, and burnt sienna) is blobbed on for the overhanging foliage in the top right-hand corner, and, slightly watered down, used also for the two grassy areas — the detail of the grass is added with a darker mixture, and little variations of colour are made with touches of yellow and extra blue in the mixture.

When the background is absolutely dry, the masking fluid is removed from the edges of the dog's shape. A yellow ochre/burnt sienna wash, stronger than the brown-yellow ground, is put on to the dog's patches, inside the hole, and around his feet for the lumps of soil.

Stage 5 — the finished painting

The black and grey detail of eye, nose, ears and paws, and quite a lot of elaborate work on the outline of the animal, defining the growth of hair and the smoother forms of the legs, are now added. Some paler grey is used to indicate shapes of the head, body and leg, and at this stage I add the brush marks defining the hair.

The masking fluid is now removed from the background, leaving the daisies sharply defined in the grass. Yellow centres are added, and a few blades of grass allowed to grow up in front of some of them.

Stage 1

Stage 2

Stage 3

Stage 4

Stage 5 — the finished painting

Greyhounds

Greyhounds are another very ancient group, bred for coursing — running down hunted animals, however swift — and capable of considerable speeds. Our own racing greyhounds show clearly the shape of the dogs: salukis, Afghan hounds, borzois, Irish wolfhounds and Scottish deerhounds are very like them under their hair, and whippets and Italian greyhounds are smaller versions of the same animal.

They are well proportioned, graceful dogs, strong, and deep-chested — essential to accommodate large powerful lungs.

The member of the group illustrated below is a saluki, the Persian greyhound, said to be scarcely changed in 5000 years. This individual has a pale creamy colour, smooth and shiny, with long wavy hair on the ears and tail, and fringes on legs and feet. A smooth thin wash is used for the body, the form indicated with deeper tones; a thin black wash over the muzzle, and details of the face, eye and nose; then wavy brush marks for the long locks of hair on ears and tail.

Running greyhound: demonstration (pages 28 & 29)

Original size: 160 x 225mm/6½ x 9in.
Paper: Mould-made Whatman 300gsm/140lb.

Stage 1

This is another subject where careful drawing must be the first consideration. A pencil outline has been used, and the background kept very simple.

Photographic reference has been used to ensure accuracy. The tongue is coloured with a thin wash of cadmium scarlet, and the eye with yellow ochre.

Stage 2

The background of pale yellow-green, mixed from pthalo-cyanine blue and cadmium lemon, is floated on to the previously wetted paper. Stronger green, with a little Payne's grey added, is put into the wet wash below the figure of the dog.

A very weak wash of yellow ochre, with a very little burnt sienna, is put over the face, the inside of the further legs, the belly, the front of the nearer thigh, and the dog's right hind foot.

Stage 3

At this stage the main colour of the dog's coat is added, using a stronger wash of yellow ochre, and blending this colour where it ends with the very pale parts already done, so that there are no hard edges between the dark and pale parts.

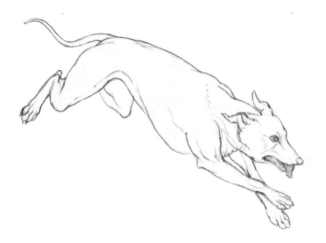

Stage 1

Stage 2

Stage 3.

Detail

Detail

This detail of the greyhound painting shows how bones, tendons and even blood-vessels show through the thin, close coat of the animal, just as they do in a thoroughbred horse. This has been conveyed by the application of darker, more sharply-edged patches of tone than those used for the broader forms on which these details lie.

Stage 4 — the finished painting

Stage 4 — the finished painting

The final building up of deep tones is done at this stage with successive washes of almost pure burnt sienna, and of black on the muzzle, neck, chest, thigh and feet. The muscles and veins are defined, and yet stronger black used for pupil, mouth, nose, whiskers and claws. Details of ears, eyes and feet are strengthened, and the pencil line built up in places with a black wash line.

Poodles

The practice of clipping poodles' coats into a pattern originated as a means of reducing interference with their movements in water. Since those more practical times, man has devised many fanciful variations on the theme; two are shown in the picture, a standard and miniature poodle; the large, black one's waves and curls are put in over a soft wash of medium black, softened at the edges, with many fine brush strokes in black and then, using opaque white, in pale grey. The little dog has his curls in similar strokes, but all in a colour slightly deeper in tone than his ground colour, a pale apricot. As always, with a long-haired dog, when I work on the important stage of preliminary drawing, I draw the inner dog first, and build out the thickness of the hair over this.

The Spitz group

These dogs are the nearest in appearance to wolves, not necessarily in size, as they range from the Eskimo dogs, which really are like wolves and which in fact have been known to interbreed with them, to the toy pomeranian. The characteristics of the group include upright pointed ears, tightly curled tails, pointed noses, and a thick springy coat.

The breed illustrated is a samoyed.

The samoyed picture is almost in monochrome, the only patch of colour is the pink tongue. Apart from the eyes, nose and mouth, the drawing consists mostly of hair — the coat is very dense and weather-resistant.

Page 32
This dog is painted almost entirely in watercolours, but soft white chalk has been used to define the plume hair of its tail and ruff. This technique can be used very successfully to realise diffuse patterns of white fur over a darker background.

ACKNOWLEDGEMENTS

Text, drawings and paintings by Sally Michel

Text, illustrations, arrangement and typography
copyright © Search Press Limited 1985

First published in Great Britain in 1985 by Search Press Limited,
Wellwood, North Farm Road, Tunbridge Wells, Kent TN2 3DR

Reprinted 1987, 1989

Much of the material in this book, text and illustrations, has
previously appeared in *Painting Animals in Watercolour* by Sally
Michel, also published by Search Press Limited.

U.S. Artists Materials Trade Distributor:
Winsor & Newton, Inc.
11, Constitution Avenue, P. O. Box 1396, Piscataway, NJ08855-1396

Canadian Distributors:
Anthes Universal Limited
341 Heart Lake Road South, Brampton, Ontario L6W 3K8

Australian Distributors:
Jasco Pty. Limited
937-941 Victoria Road, West Ryde, N.S.W. 2114

New Zealand Distributors:
Caldwell Wholesale Ltd
Wellington and Auckland

UK ISBN 0 85532 559 3

Made and printed in Spain by A. G. Elkar, S. Coop.
Autonomía, 71 - 48012-Bilbao Spain.